How to Pray

Lessons from the Lord's Prayer

TIMOTHY J.E. CROSS
B.A. (Hons), B.D. (Hons), P.G.C.E., Th.D., Dip.Th.

AMBASSADOR

BELFAST, NORTHERN IRELAND
GREENVILLE, USA

How to Pray
© Copyright 2003 Timothy J. E. Cross

ISBN 1   84030   138   4

Ambassador Publications
a division of
Ambassador Productions Ltd.
Providence House
Ardenlee Street,
Belfast,
BT6 8QJ
Northern Ireland
www.ambassador-productions.com

Emerald House
427 Wade Hampton Blvd.
Greenville
SC 29609, USA
www.emeraldhouse.com

Contents

Dedication

To Lynn and Peggy Schuster -
esteemed friends in the Faith and in the pew.

The 'Lord's Prayer'

Our Father Who art in heaven,
Hallowed be Thy name.
Thy kingdom come,
Thy will be done,
On earth as it is in heaven
Give us this day our daily bread;
And forgive us our debts,
As we also have forgiven our debtors;
And lead us not into temptation,
But deliver us from evil.
For Thine is the kingdom and the power
and the glory, for ever. Amen

(Matthew 6: 9-13).

Preface

When I lived in Belfast, N. Ireland, the church of which I was a member held a prayer meeting every Thursday evening at 8.00 pm. Attending this prayer meeting was always a great blessing. The hour or so with God's people proved to be a real 'spiritual haven' from all the difficulties, dangers and disappointments through which I was living at that time.

Although a few years have passed, and I now find myself living the other side of the Irish Sea, I still recall vividly that another regular attender at our Thursday prayer meeting was one Mr Sampson. Mr Sampson was a godly Christian in his eighties, who has since gone to be with Christ. When I knew him, he was slightly deaf and struggling with various physical 'aches and pains'. Yet his face seemed to radiate with the joy of the Lord.

To hear Mr Sampson pray really was 'something else'. Never before had I heard such fluency, beauty of cadence and a sense of both reverence for and intimacy with the Lord. Here was a man talking to none less than Almighty God. Mr Sampson's prayers often lifted the meeting to a different level. When he said his 'Amen' and sat down, invariably there was silence for a while. We were all afraid to follow him, lest the poverty and paucity of our praying was shown up in contrast with his. Oh to be able to pray like Mr Sampson!

The above is similar to an incident in Luke 11. When the disciples overheard the Lord Jesus praying, they too felt that they had barely reached the kindergarten stage in the school of prayer. How they longed to be able to pray like the Lord Jesus. *He was praying in a certain place, and when He ceased, one of His disciples said to Him, 'Lord, teach us to pray, as John taught his disciples'* (Luke 11:1).

We are grateful for this request, as it led to the Lord bequeathing to us the most perfect prayer for imperfect people. The prayer is recorded for us twice in Scripture, in Luke 11:2-4 and also a little fuller in Matthew 5:9-13. This perfect prayer has come to be known as 'The Lord's Prayer'. 'The Lord's Prayer' though is actually something of a misnomer. The Lord certainly taught this prayer, but had no need of praying this prayer Himself. Technically, it would be better to term it 'The Disciples' Prayer' - the true 'Lord's Prayer' being recorded in John 17.

But what a prayer is this 'Disciples' Prayer'. No better prayer can be prayed by a sinner saved by grace. It is also the ideal prayer for those who find praying a bit of a struggle at times - it is thus the ideal prayer for us all.

In the following pages, I seek to shed fresh light on this ancient prayer. Its words are certainly among some of the most well known words of the Bible, and yet familiarity has its dangers. The phrases can roll off our tongues without any thought or heart. Our knowledge of its words can blunt us to its meaning and blind us to its wonder. This should not be so, even though it sometimes is:-

> I often say my prayers
> But do I really pray?
> And do the wishes of my heart
> Go with the words I say
>
> I may as well kneel down
> And worship gods of stone
> As offer to the living God
> A prayer of words alone
>
> For words without the heart
> The Lord will never hear
> Nor will He to those lips attend
> Whose prayers are not sincere

Lord, teach me what I need
And TEACH ME HOW TO PRAY
Nor let me ask Thee for Thy grace
Not meaning what I say.

If what I have written in the following pages leads to helping you to 'really pray', that is, to pray the 'Disciples' Prayer' with increased understanding and joy, my intention in taking up this labour will have been pleasurably fulfilled.

Joining you in the school of prayer then, I too say *Lord, teach us to pray.* May the Spirit of God deliver us from formalism and praying the model prayer in a merely perfunctory manner. May we take ever more delight in the duty and joy of prayer and never lose the wonder of the relationship which we have with God through our Lord and Saviour Jesus Christ.

Lord, teach us to pray.

Timothy J. E. Cross
Barry
South Wales

1

ADOPTION
Our Father Who art in heaven . . .

What doth the Preface of the Lord's Prayer teach us?

The Preface of the Lord's Prayer (which is, OUR FATHER WHICH ART IN HEAVEN), teacheth us to draw near to God with all holy reverence and confidence, as children to a father, able and ready to help us, and that we should pray with and for others (Shorter Catechism, Q. 100).

'What is a Christian? The answer can be answered in many ways, but the richest answer I know is that a Christian is one who has God as Father.' So said James Packer in his classic book *Knowing God* (p.225). Packer affirms here that knowing and enjoying God as our loving heavenly Father is integral to Biblical Christianity - and his affirmation is right in-line with the Lord's Jesus's teaching us that we should address God as *Our Father Who art in heaven.* Similarly, the Apostle Paul - one of the Christian Faith's greatest ever exponents - also taught that true Christianity involves knowing God as Father. Paul could write: *When we cry 'Abba! Father!' it is the Spirit Himself bearing witness with our spirit that we are children of God* (Romans 8:15,16). *And because you are sons, God has sent the Spirit of His Son into our hearts, crying 'Abba! Father'* (Galatians 4:6).

Think for one moment of the ideal human father - even if it is doubtful if such a father exists in a fallen world! An ideal human father conjures up words such as love, affection, availability, provision, protection, wisdom, guidance, trustworthiness, understanding, dependability, and an over-all total commitment to his children's earthly and eternal welfare. If we then were to multiply these words by infinity, we would almost begin to approach what it is to have God as our Father. The amazing fact is though, that, according to the Bible, knowing God as our Father is and can be a reality and not a fantasy. In the God of heaven we have an infinitely perfect Father. Once in this secure relationship, it is inconceivable that anything can ever go wrong with us in time or eternity. And so the model prayer begins by addressing God as *Our Father Who art in heaven.*

What though do the Scriptures in general, and the Lord Jesus's teaching in particular mean when it describes God as 'Father'?

i. 'Father' reminds us of God's authority

Biblical society was 'patriarchal'. In Bible days the father 'ruled the roost.' Unpalatable though it may seem to us, Deuteronomy 21:18 ff. shows how in those days, a father was entitled to have a rebellious son stoned to death. A father then was a figure of authority, hence the commandments *Honour your father and your mother* (Exodus 20:12), *Children, obey your parents in everything* . . . (Colossians 3:19).

As our Father, God is to be honoured and obeyed. In Malachi 1:6, God Himself asks *If then I am a Father, where is My honour?* If an earthly father has a degree of power and authority in his family, in God we meet One Who is all-powerful and One Who is the Ultimate authority. He is God *Most High* (Psalm 92:1). Under God, our earthly fathers are responsible for our lives. Humanly speaking, we would not be here if it were not for them. The God of heaven, in complete contrast, is our Father Who is responsible for creating and sustaining all things. *The LORD is the everlasting God, the creator of the ends of the earth. He does not grow faint or weary, His understanding is unsearchable* (Isaiah 40:28).

ii. 'Father' speaks of God's affection

There is something special, unique and exclusive about a father-child relationship. A father-child relationship is in a totally different league from, say, the relationship between an employer and an employee, or a teacher and a pupil or even between a man and his 'mates'.

Knowing God as Father reminds us that He loves us with an everlasting love, and is committed to our eternal welfare. *As a father pities his children, so the LORD pities those who fear Him* (Psalm 103:13). *We know that in everything God works for good with those who love Him, who are called according to His purpose* (Romans 8:28). Knowing the love of God nurtures in us a love for God and a trust in God in response. *We love because He first loved us* (1 John 4:19). The unchanging God is infinitely worthy of our trust.

In the 'Sermon on the Mount', the Lord Jesus expands a little more on the Fatherly love of God - a love which gives us a great incentive to pray to Him. The Lord employed the method of contrast in his teaching. He contrasted the love of a human father which accomplishes some things with that of our heavenly Father which accomplishes everything. *Or what man of you, if his son asks him for bread, will give him a stone? Or if he asks for a fish will give him a serpent? If you then, who are evil, know how to give good gifts to your children, how much more will your Father Who is in heaven give good things to those who ask Him* (Matthew 7:9,10).

iii 'Father' reminds us that God is truly awesome

Notice that God is not just our Father, but *Our Father . . . in heaven.* This reminds us of God's infinite greatness - His royal high-ness and dazzling glory. *Thus says the LORD: 'Heaven is My throne and earth is My footstool . . .*(Isaiah 66:1). Our Father is *the high and lofty One Who inhabits eternity, Whose name is Holy* (Isaiah 57:15).

When we pray to our Father in heaven, we are taking things both literally and metaphorically 'to the top'. There is none higher or greater or more powerful than God. What a privilege then it is to pray to *Our*

Father . . . in heaven. It is the highest privilege we can ever have on earth. It is a privilege so great and outstanding, that it would be inconceivable and impossible were it not for the grace of God reaching down to us first.

Our Adoption

Our Father . . . The address *Our Father* suggests a reciprocal relationship: God is our Father, and we are His children, and the love and affection, although unequal, is mutual. The question is - Can anyone take this prayer on their lips? Can anybody automatically call God 'Father' and enjoy all the blessings and benefits which flow from His Fatherhood? These are crucial questions, for presumption here is deadly.

The prayer which begins *Our Father* is a distinctly and distinctively Christian prayer. Only Christians may pray it. The prayer was given as a guide to Jesus's disciples then and now. The testimony of Scripture is clear when it teaches that no one can pray this prayer automatically, as, by nature, we are not the children of God, and God is not our Father. Hence, we will have no desire or ability to truly pray this prayer apart from the grace of God. Scripture teaches that because of our sin, *we were by nature children of wrath, like the rest of mankind* (Ephesians 2:3). By nature, prayer to God is impossible. By God's supernatural intervention, prayer is wonderfully and actually possible. By nature, we are separated from God and need to be reconciled to Him. Naturally, we are sinners under God's wrath, and His wrath needs to be averted if all is to be well with our souls. By nature, we are out of God's family, and if we are to ever know an intimate relationship with God, we need to be born again, and brought into the family of God. . . The Gospel proclaims that all these desperate needs have been met in the giving of God's Son, and His death on the cross for our sins. It is through the cross that we are reconciled to God. It is through the cross that the wrath of God is pacified, and it is through the cross that we may be adopted into the family of God, and so be able to genuinely call Him 'Father'.

Adoption is one of the key ways in which the Bible understands salvation. A Christian is one who has been 'adopted by grace' as much as 'saved by grace.' We are not naturally members of the family of God - the blessing is a supernatural one. It is divine and not human. It is not there at our birth, but only when by God's grace we undergo a new birth and are born again. It is only through Christ, the unique Son of God, that the children of wrath can ever become the children of God. *But to all who received Him, who believed in His name, He gave power to become children of God; who were born, not of blood nor of the will of the flesh nor of the will of man, but of God* (John 1:12,13).

'Adoption is an act of God's free grace whereby we are received into the number and have a right to all the privileges of the sons of God' (*Shorter Catechism*, Q.34).

That the God of heaven should ever take sinners into His family, and bestow on them the full rights of sons, is a never ending source of amazement and praise. *See what love the Father has given us, that we should be called children of God; and so we are* (1 John 3:1).

O how shall I the goodness tell
Father, which Thou to me hast showed?
That I, a child of wrath and hell
I should be called a child of God
Should know, should feel my sins forgiven
Blest with this antepast of heaven.

Family Life

Family life is good for us. It has its privileges for sure, but it also has its responsibilities. We receive much, but we also have to 'give and take' too. Family life is a check and counter-balance against the ingrained selfishness that mars us all.

The Christian life is a family life as well. No one can be a Christian in total isolation, for once we are saved, we are adopted into God's family, and thus become a member of the *household of God* (1 Timothy 3:15). God becomes our Father when Christ is our Saviour, but also, other Christians now become our brothers and sisters. There can only now be a mutual concern amongst 'God's siblings' - those united by Christ's blood-tie of redemption. And so the model prayer begins <u>Our</u> *Father.* The prayer is certainly suitable for praying in private, and yet how fitting it is to be prayed together in our gatherings for public worship too. The prayer knows nothing of 'me and my' but only of 'us and our'. The prayer thus enhances our Christian fellowship and the relationship which we have with both God in heaven and our fellow believers on earth.

Family comes first! *Bear one another's burdens, and so fulfil the law of Christ* (Galatians 6:2). *So then, as we have opportunity, let us do good to all men, and especially to those who are of the household of faith* (Galatians 6:10).

The wonder of it all

Our Father who art in heaven . . . And so begins the model prayer. Knowing God as our loving Father in heaven encourages us to pray to Him and to worship Him - as it also encourages us to trust Him and rely on Him to meet all our needs.

Our Father . . . Perhaps the words do roll of our tongues too easily and unthinkingly. The privilege though of having the God of heaven as our concerned and committed Father just cannot be surpassed.

> All those that are justified, God vouchsafeth, in and for His only Son Jesus Christ, to make partakers of the grace of adoption, by which they are taken into the number, and enjoy the liberties and privileges of the children of God, have His name put upon them, receive the spirit of adoption, have access to the throne of grace with boldness, are enabled to say Abba, Father, are pitied, protected, provided for and chastened by Him, as by a Father: yet never cast off, but sealed to the day of redemption; and inherit the promises, as heirs of everlasting salvation (Chapter XII, *Westminster Confession).*

2

ADORATION
Hallowed be Thy name.

What do we pray for in the first petition?

*In the first petition, (which is HALLOWED BE THY NAME)
we pray, that God would enable us and others to glorify Him
in all that whereby He maketh Himself known; and that He
would dispose all things to His own glory*
(*Shorter Catechism*, Q. 101).

Getting our priorities right

We note at the outset that the first petition of the model prayer is
concerned with God and not with ourselves. Pressing though our needs
are, the perfect prayer would have us focus on God and His glory first of
all. The emphasis here is in-line with the whole Bible. The Lord Jesus
was well aware of our need of material things, yet He stressed *Seek first*

His (God's) kingdom and His righteousness, and all these things shall be yours as well (Matthew 6:33). The first and foremost commandment is likewise concerned with God's honour and glory. God commands: *You shall have no other gods before Me* (Exodus 20:3).

What does it mean?

In this first petition of the perfect prayer, we pray that God would enable us to hallow His name. To hallow means 'to set apart as holy'. God's 'name' refers to the revelation of Himself - His very person and character. Hallowing God's name therefore means that we acknowledge that God is God, and walk before Him in reverence and godly fear all the days of our life. In this petition though, we do not only pray that human beings would glorify God, but also that events would too. Looking out and around us, we might fear that people and events are far from honouring God. The age in which we live seems to be far gone in ungodliness and almost total secularism. Scripture though affirms that the goal of history is the unsurpassed glory of God. God Himself will see that this is achieved, and nothing at all can hinder or thwart Him from achieving His purpose. *To Him be glory for ever* (Romans 11:36). *As I live, says the Lord, every knee shall bow to Me, and every tongue shall give praise to God* (Romans 14:11).

The Holiness of God

'Holiness' encapsulates the very God-ness of God. He is an incomparable God, infinitely different from us, the creatures He has created. God is in a category all on His Own, and He has no rivals at all.

> There is but one only, living, and true God, who is infinite in being and perfection, a most pure spirit, invisible, without body, parts or passions; immutable, immense, eternal, incomprehensible, almighty, most wise, most holy, most free, most absolute; working all things according to the counsel of His own immutable and most righteous will, for His own glory . . . (*Westminster Confession,* chapter II).

Scripture affirms that the holiness, separateness, and infinite difference of God is one of His primary characteristics:-

Holy, holy, holy, is the Lord God Almighty, Who was and is and is to come (Revelation 4:8).

Thy way, O God, is holy. What God is great like our God? (Psalm 77:13).

Who is like Thee, O LORD, among the gods? Who is like Thee, majestic in holiness (Exodus 15:11).

Who is a God like Thee, pardoning iniquity and passing over transgression for the remnant of His inheritance? He does not retain His anger for ever because He delights in steadfast love (Micah 7:18).

The holiness of God reminds us that God is not to be trifled with. Perhaps the public worship of the church has become a little too casual in recent years . . . A true sense of God's holiness would change all this in an instant. God's holiness has the effect of making us bow humbly in the dust before Him.

The Purity of God

Bound up with God's holiness, is His indescribable, immeasurable, immaculate and terrifying moral purity. It is difficult for us ever to conceive of this, for our minds are tainted by sin. God though is totally unlike us. *God is light and in Him there is no darkness at all* (1 John 1:5). *Thou . . . art of purer eyes than to behold evil and canst not look on wrong* (Habakkuk 1:13).

The holiness of God then is most formidable and intimidating. The prophet Isaiah was typical of 'every man'. No sooner had the the prophet Isaiah sensed something of God's holiness, than he cried out: *Woe is me! For I am lost; for I am a man of unclean lips, and I dwell in the midst of a people of unclean lips; for my eyes have seen the King, the LORD of hosts!* (Isaiah 6:5). How then can we ever hope to have fellowship with this God? He is so far above and beyond us. Our sin makes us totally unfit and unsuited for His holy presence. The answer of the Bible is the Gospel of our Lord Jesus Christ. *There is one God and there is One Mediator between God and men, the Man Christ Jesus* (1 Timothy 2:5). The hymn writer put it so well in the following hymn - a hymn of praise to God for the fact that unholy creatures may yet enjoy fellowship with their holy Creator. They may do so because of the amazing love and mercy of God in providing His Own Son to die as a sacrifice for our sins:-

Eternal light! Eternal light!
How pure the soul must be
When placed within Thy searching sight
It shrinks not, but with calm delight
Can live and look on Thee

O how shall I, whose native sphere
Is dark, whose mind is dim
Before the ineffable appear
And on my naked spirit bear
The uncreated beam?

There is a way for man to rise
To that sublime abode
An offering and a sacrifice
A Holy Spirit's energies
An Advocate with God

These, these prepare us for the sight
Of holiness above
The sons of ignorance and night
May dwell with the eternal Light
Through the eternal love.

Hallowing God's Name

Hallowed by Thy name. The God of the Bible is a holy God. The God of the Bible is to be acknowledged as a holy God, with our lips and with our lives. The God of the Bible will one day manifest Himself as the incomparably holy God that He is. The realisation of this drives us to our knees. It makes us seek God's pardon for the many times we have not hallowed His name, and for all the dark areas of our lives that are an affront to His holiness. The petition also makes us seek God's grace that we might be enabled to hallow His name as we ought - or as much as it is possible for redeemed sinners so to do.

Hallowing God's name involves worshipping God, that is, extolling His great worth. Worship gives verbal expression to the inward, God-ward reverence of our hearts. The Psalms are a great aid in this respect. The Psalms bring our minds back into focusing on the true God, and give a verbal articulation to the worship of our hearts which is unsurpassed. The Psalms may be considered as the divinely inspired hymn book of the Bible. Psalms such as the following truly hallow God's name:-

Great is the LORD, and greatly to be praised; He is to be feared above all gods. For all the gods of the peoples are idols; but the LORD made the heavens. Honour and majesty are before Him; strength and beauty are in His sanctuary (Psalm 96:6).

Hallowing God's name also involves seeking to please God in all that we do - in thought, word and deed - and seeking His grace to obey His commandments. Micah summarised 'true religion' in the sight of God like this: *He has shown you, O man, what is good; and what does the LORD require of you but to do justice, and to love kindness, and to walk humbly with your God?* (Micah 6:8).

Finally, hallowing God's name involves praying to God that He will save and sanctify His people, build the church of the Lord Jesus Christ, and fulfil His eternal purpose of grace, and so glorify His name in all the earth. May God's name be hallowed - *hallowed be Thy name.*

Holy, holy, holy! Thee
One Jehovah evermore
Father, Son and Spirit we
Dust and ashes, would adore
Lightly by the world esteemed
From that world by Thee redeemed
Say we here with glad accord
Holy, holy, holy Lord

Holy, holy, holy! all
Heaven's triumphant choirs shall sing
When the ransomed nations fall

At the footstool of their King
Then shall saints and seraphim
Harps and voices, swell one hymn
Blending in sublime accord
Holy, holy, holy Lord!

3

ANTICIPATION
Thy kingdom come.

What do we pray for in the second petition?

*In the second petition (which is THY KINGDOM COME) we
pray that Satan's kingdom may be destroyed; and that the
kingdom of grace may be advanced, ourselves and others brought
into it, and kept in it; and that the kingdom of glory may be
hastened* (Shorter Catechism, Q. 102).

Opening words often set the tone for what is to follow. The Lord Jesus
opened His public ministry with these words: *'The time is fulfilled, and
the kingdom of God is at hand; repent, and believe the Gospel'* (Mark
1:15) - and so we see how central 'the kingdom of God' is to the
Scriptures.

Here in the United Kingdom, in June of 2002, we celebrated the
Golden Jubilee of Her Majesty, Queen Elizabeth II. Great Britain is a

Monarchy - we are ruled by a Queen, and not governed by a President. The Kingdom of God though refers to the rule and reign of none less than Almighty God Himself.

God, however, it may be objected, has always reigned. Indeed He has. He is the King of kings. The Psalmist was able to say of Him: *Thy kingdom is an everlasting kingdom, and Thy dominion endures throughout all generations* (Psalm 145:13). The Kingdom of God then, more specifically, refers to the personal experience of the eternal reign of God in human life and hearts. It is for this that we pray when we pray *Thy kingdom come.* Here we are actually praying for the Blessing of all blessings - to know and enjoy being ruled and governed by the God Who is love (1 John 4:8).

Scripture shows that the Kingdom of God is inextricably bound up with the Person and Work of the Lord Jesus Christ, God's eternal Son. One of His Messianic offices is that of King. 'Christ executeth the office of a king in subduing us to Himself, in ruling and defending us, and in restraining and conquering all His and our enemies' (*Shorter Catechism,* Q. 26). He came into the world to inaugurate the eternal, saving reign of God - and He will come again in due course to consummate the kingdom of God.

> Jesus shall reign where'er the sun
> Doth its successive journeys run
> His kingdom stretch from shore to shore
> Till moons shall wax and wane no more
>
> Blessings abound where'er He reigns
> The prisoner leaps to lose his chains
> The weary find eternal rest
> And all the sons of want are blest.

Let us then look in further detail as to what the Kingdom of God involves. We should then be able to pray this second petition a little more intelligently:-

1. Enjoying God's kingdom entails a change of rulers

A non-Christian, however 'nice' and however outwardly

respectable, would not take it too kindly if they were told that they are currently ruled by Satan - but Scripture teaches that this is clearly the case. John, writing to Christians clearly stated this 'them and us' position: *We know that we are of God, and the whole world is in the power of the evil one* (1 John 5:19). Salvation, it follows, involves being delivered from the power of Satan. Writing to the Christians at Colossi, Paul rejoiced so: *He (God) has delivered us from the dominion of darkness and transferred us to the kingdom of His beloved Son* (Colossians 1:13). Paul actually viewed his life-work and vocation as being an instrument of divine deliverance - a means whereby people would have a change of ruler, and move from Satan's destructive kingdom into God's glorious kingdom. God commissioned Paul directly to go to the Gentiles *to open their eyes, that they may turn from darkness to light and from the power of Satan to God, that they may receive forgiveness of sins . . .* (Acts 26:18).

Looking around us today, we fear that Satan's kingdom has many citizens. Proportionately few, it seems, submit to God's saving rule. The Bible explains this starkly: *In their case the god of this world has blinded the minds of the unbelievers, to keep them from seeing the light of the gospel of the glory of Christ* (2 Corinthians 4:4). We should never despair of anyone though, but rather pray to God that His kingdom will come in their lives - that He will intervene in saving power in their souls and perform a miracle of grace. The world is full of unlikely converts! No one is too far gone for omnipotence. *God may perhaps grant that they will repent and come to know the truth, and that they may escape from the snare of the devil, after being captured by him to do his will* (2 Timothy 2:25,26).

2. We enter God's kingdom when we believe the Gospel of Christ

The Lord Jesus once stated *'Truly, truly, I say to you, unless one is born anew, he cannot see the kingdom of God '*(John 3:3). The converse of this is that once we have been born again, we enter into the glorious kingdom of God there and then. The kingdom of God therefore is synonymous with the gift of eternal life which only Jesus can give. Once we are enabled by grace to trust in Jesus, and His death on the cross for our sins, we receive the gift of eternal life - the forgiveness of sins, peace with God, fellowship with God and a home in heaven by and by.

The free gift of God is eternal life in Christ Jesus our Lord (Romans 6:23). Jesus keeps His promises! *'Truly, truly, I say to you, he who hears My Word and believes Him Who sent Me, has eternal life; he does not come into judgement, but has passed from death to life'* (John 5:24).

Eternal life therefore may begin now. Whilst I am a citizen of the United Kingdom, I am also a citizen of the kingdom of heaven! I am a child of the King! *our commonwealth is in heaven* (Philippians 3:20).

In praying the petition *Thy kingdom come* therefore, we are praying for the triumph of the Gospel in this world and the extension of God's glorious kingdom of grace. We are praying that men and women, and boys and girls would come to know the saving power of God and submit to the Lordship of Christ. We, of course are powerless in and of ourselves to extend God's kingdom. He alone is the One *Who calls you into His own kingdom and glory* (1 Thessalonians 2:12). Yet this petition paradoxically exhorts us to pray that God would cause His work to prosper in the area where we live and beyond, and that He would accomplish His saving purposes by His Word and by His Spirit to the blessing of souls and the glory of His name. The kingdom of God was a priority in Paul's prayers - and he invited others to join in this holy petition too. It is a petition which Christians will always pray, until that great Day when King Jesus will return in power and glory, and our prayers will be finally answered. *Finally, brethren, pray for us, that the Word of the Lord may speed on and triumph, as it did among you* (1 Thessalonians 3:1).

3. God's kingdom will yet come in all its fulness

When we pray *Thy kingdom come*, we are praying a prayer which has both a present and a future facet to it. God's kingdom is yet to come fully - but fully come it surely will. The goal of history is the kingdom of God. God's kingdom will be gloriously consummated when the King comes to earth in power and great glory, i.e. at the Second Coming of the Lord Jesus Christ. At the Second Coming of Christ, all that is incompatible with God's kingdom will be eradicated, and His rule of perfect righteousness and peace will be established for ever.

In the last book of the Bible, the book of Revelation, John was given a prophetic foresight into the end of time, and the wrapping up of world history. His inspired words concerning the time when *The kingdom of this world has become the kingdom of our Lord and of His Christ, and He shall reign for ever* (Revelation 11:15), have thrilled and heartened Christians in all ages. It points us to the time when the petition *Thy kingdom come* will be fully answered by God in a way more glorious than we can ever imagine. The kingdom of God is the pinnacle of blessing and so we pray *Thy kingdom come* with heightened anticipation. It is for God's glorious kingdom that we wait. It is for God's glorious kingdom that we eagerly and earnestly desire. It is for God's glorious kingdom that we pray. Our prayers will be answered. God's kingdom will surely come in God's good time. *According to His promise we wait for new heavens and a new earth in which righteousness dwells* (2 Peter 3:13).

Maranatha!

One of the earliest ever prayers of the Christian church was *Maranatha. Our Lord come!*(1 Corinthians 16:22). The last but one verse of the whole Bible contains the earnest plea *Come, Lord Jesus!* (Revelation 22:20). Christians therefore will continue to pray to God *Thy kingdom come* - that He would further the rule of the Gospel of grace in this world, and that He would hasten the coming kingdom of King Jesus in all its glory, to the praise and honour of His glorious name. *Thy kingdom come.*

> Thy kingdom come, O God
> Thy rule, O Christ, begin!
> Break with Thine iron rod
> The tyranny of sin
>
> Where is Thy reign of peace
> And purity and love?
> When shall all hatred cease
> As in the realms above?
>
> When comes the promised time
> That war shall be no more?
> Oppression, lust and crime
> Shall flee Thy face before

We pray Thee, Lord, arise
And come in Thy great might
Revive our longing eyes
Which languish in Thy sight.

4

ASPIRATION
Thy will be done, on earth as it is in heaven.

What do we pray for in the third petition?

*In the third petition, (which is, THY WILL BE DONE IN
EARTH, AS IT IS IN HEAVEN), we pray that God, by His
grace, would make us able and willing to know, obey and submit
to His will in all things, as the angels do in heaven*
(*Shorter Catechism*, Q.103).

A petition that will be answered

In praying to God *Thy will be done . . .* we face a paradox similar to the
one when we pray *Thy kingdom come.* Just as God's kingdom will surely
come - whether we pray for it or not - so, ultimately, God's will will be
universally done - whether we pray for it or not. God's will will prevail.
God will have His Own way for He is Almighty God. He *accomplishes*

all things according to the counsel of His will (Ephesians 1:11). He has pronounced *'My counsel shall stand, and I will accomplish all My purpose'* (Isaiah 46:10). Nothing can thwart or hinder God's will: *'I work and who can hinder it?'* (Isaiah 43:13). *The LORD of hosts has sworn: 'As I have planned, so shall it be, and as I have purposed, so shall it stand'* (Isaiah 14:24).

Thy will is best

In Romans 12:2 *the will of God* is described as *what is good and acceptable and perfect.* This being so, how we should long to be living in the centre of the will of God. Our Maker, being infinite in wisdom and love, knows what is the best for us. Conversely, to go against our Maker's will would be to go against the grain. As a car is made to drive on the road and not sail on the sea, and as a light bulb is made to emit light and not to be eaten, so we are designed to do the will of God. Not doing the will of God is a sure recipe for unhappiness. How earnest and sincere should we be therefore when we pray this third petition: *Thy will be done.* The Psalms contain similar aspirations:- *Make me to know Thy ways, O LORD, teach me Thy paths* (Psalm 25:4). *Teach me Thy way, O LORD* (Psalm 86:11).

Teach me Thy way, O Lord
Teach me Thy way
Thy gracious will afford
Teach me Thy way
Help me to walk aright
More by faith, less by sight
Lead me with heavenly light
Teach me Thy way.

Discerning God's will

The crucial question is:'How may I know the will of God for my life?' The answer to this crucial question may be gained by considering 1. God's Word, and 2. God's Providence.

1. God's Word

As the Bible is the Word of God written - *All Scripture is inspired by God* (2 Timothy 3:16) - it is through reading the Bible that we discover the will of God for our lives - what He expects of us. In the Holy Bible we have been given our Maker's instruction manual. What an inestimable privilege it is to have a Book which owes its origin to God Himself. God has not left us in the dark. He has revealed His mind to us. The Holy Scriptures are nothing less than a revelation of the mind of the eternal God for the eternal blessing of man. A desire to know and do the will of God therefore can only be matched by an equal desire to carefully, prayerfully and systematically study the pages of the Scriptures from Genesis 1:1 to Revelation 22:21. Daily reading of the Bible is the norm for a Christian. We would no more miss this than we would omit brushing our teeth. When we read though, we pray that God will illuminate the pages to us - *Open my eyes, that I may behold wondrous things out of Thy law* (Psalm 119:18). We also pray that God would give us grace to obey what we read - to be as obedient as can be expected for a redeemed sinner to be.

God's Word therefore reveals God's will. Remembering God's sovereignty over all things though, we note that God's will is also known by considering:-

2. God's Providence

If the Scriptures are the revealed will of God, then God's providence is the gradual unfolding of His secret will. *The secret things belong to the LORD our God; but the things that are revealed belong to us and to our children for ever, that we may do all the words of this law* (Deuteronomy 29:29).

Whilst the will of God, as revealed in the Bible, is binding on all, the will of God for any particular individual's life differs from case to case. We only discover the latter will by stepping out in faith, dedicating ourselves to God, and with careful thought asking Him: *'What shall I do, Lord?'* (Acts 22:10).

Careful thought is certainly necessary if we are to do the will of God. We are all unique. God has made us in an individual and particular way. We cannot ignore our own inclinations, even if we have to ensure that our inclinations do not go against anything which is expressly prohibited in the Bible. We also have to consider the particular gifts, talents and abilities that God has given us, and how they may be used for His glory and the benefit of others. Our gifts may be with people, things or concepts. Our abilities may be scientific, artistic or mechanical. We may be endowed with a mighty intellect which grasps concepts at the first explanation. Or our abilities may be more in a practical line, working with our hands. The will of God also differs if we are male or female. The contemporary world preaches the absolute equality of the sexes. The Bible though stresses that although the genders are complementary, there is yet a distinction between male and female - *male and female He created them* (Genesis 1:27). Hence some jobs and roles are more appropriate to one gender than the other. Then there are also our circumstances. The Bible teaches that these are not accidental but divinely ordained. Paul could say how *a wide door for effective ministry has opened to me* . . . (1 Corinthians 16:9). It is the sovereign Lord Who leads us and guides us and prepares us for what He has prepared for us, once we have been saved and have a longing to do His will.

The disappointments of life

Consider the following cases - cases which are not unusual:-

Here is a Christian young man, eager to do the will of God. His prayers are earnest and sincere. 'May Thy will be done in my life, O Lord.' He is trained and qualified in a particular sphere. His inclinations are here too. But all this notwithstanding, no openings come for him in this avenue. He performs well at job interviews, but the job always goes to someone else. He eventually takes a job in another field, and lives with his feelings of disappointment and unfulfillment.

Here is a Christian who enjoys sport. The recreation is a welcome antidote to sitting at a desk in an office for eight hours a day. It also gives him contacts and bridges for the Gospel of Christ. Overnight though, he develops a chronic injury which curtails his enjoyment of physical activity for good. Initially, it feels like a part of him has died. Being honest, he would rather things were other than they were.

Here is a Christian lady in her late twenties. She knows from the Bible that monogamous marriage is the will of the Lord. The wedding of two believers has God's stamp of approval on it. She longs to meet a compatible Christian man, and have a church based wedding and then set up home together 'til death us do part.' She suffers from pangs of loneliness - pangs which are not helped by the gradual marrying off of all her close contemporaries. How she hopes and prays for the physical and spiritual companionship which a suitable Christian man would give her - but no such man comes her way . . .

Most of us have known perplexities similar to the above. They remind us that we are not in control of our lives and circumstances. God is. What do we do in such situations?

Amidst the perplexities, pains and puzzles of this life though, we still pray *Thy will be done* - and seek God's all-sufficient grace to live with what He sends our way, and live with what He seemingly withholds from us. Scripture teaches us that our God is too wise to make mistakes, too loving to be unkind, and too powerful to be hindered in His purposes. Those who see the hand of God in everything can leave everything in the hand of God. There is a passive aspect to the will of God as well as an active one. In many cases, passively submitting to the will of God can be harder than actively doing it. The Bible tells of the passive will of God as well as His will which we actively do and obey. When Eli heard traumatic news he was enabled to say: *'It is the LORD; let Him do what seems good to Him'* (1 Samuel 3:18). Paul's friends once found God's plans for Paul very painful to accept. They begged and pleaded for him to act other than the way he intended. Acts 21:14 though pointedly records: A*nd when he would not be persuaded, we ceased and said, 'The will of the Lord be done.'*

The Saviour and God's Will: Gethsemene

Jesus once said of Himself: *'My food is to do the will of Him Who sent Me, and to accomplish His work'* (John 4:34). He also said: *'Lo, I have come to do Thy will, O God,' as it is written of Me in the roll of the book* (Hebrews 10:7). Dare we ever say that even the sinless Saviour struggled with the passive will of God? Reverently, we suggest that this was so. Naturally, He shrank from Calvary, and drinking the cup of suffering that Calvary entailed. But He submitted to it. The Bible shows how He brought His will in-line with the will of His Father, so that our redemption could be wrought. In Gethsemane, Christ prayed: *'My Father, if it be possible, let this cup pass from Me; nevertheless, not as I will but as Thou wilt'* (Matthew 26:39). It is good to recall this when we struggle with the passive will of God. Calvary is the supreme example of doing both the active and passive will of God. The Lord Jesus *humbled Himself and became obedient unto death, even death on a cross* (Philippians 2:8). Truly, *We have not a high priest Who is unable to sympathise with our weaknesses* (Hebrews 4:15).

Thy will be done. The will of God is plain - it is revealed in the Bible. Paradoxically though, the will of God can also seem mysterious to us, at any one particular time. God, however, knows what He is doing when He is working out His will. *We know that in everything God works for good with those who love Him* (Romans 8:28). *We walk by faith, not by sight* (2 Corinthians 5:7). *Now I know in part; then I shall understand fully, even as I have been fully understood* (1 Corinthians 13:12). We can be sure that in the light of eternity, we will not wish that the will of God had been anything other than it was.

Heaven on Earth

Notice, finally, that the full line of this fourth petition of the perfect prayer says *Thy will be done <u>on earth as it is in heaven.</u>*

In heaven, God's will is done perfectly, to the glory of His name and the joy of those who do it. Psalm 103:20 speaks of God's *angels . . . who do His Word, hearkening to the voice of His Word.* Doing the will of God therefore is a little bit of heaven on earth. Doing God's will is a foretaste of the coming kingdom of God, for in God's kingdom His subjects love to obey His will, and are able to fulfil it to perfection, unhindered and unhandicapped by sin. When God's kingdom comes, His will will certainly be done, as all His creatures own His sway, and all rebels against Him are banished to the outer darkness.

The joy of God's will

Thy will be done O God *on earth as it is in heaven.* A Christian longs to do God's will, and a Christian prays that God's will will be done. *God is love* (1 John 4:8), so not doing God's will, that is, not being the people He would have us be and not doing what He would have us do, means that we will be missing out very badly on the very best. Such is a sure formula for frustration. Yet this being said, no one on earth except the sinless Lord Jesus Christ and Adam before the Fall has obeyed God's will perfectly. Sin has infected us totally - our minds, emotions and our wills. The Christian however need not be unduly discouraged. Better days are ahead! When our redemption is complete, then we will be able to obey God's will as we should. *I am sure that He Who began a good work in you will bring it to completion at the day of Jesus Christ* (Philippians 1:6).

The redeemed in glory certainly do God's will. They delight in His service, and do it free from sin, fatigue and all that hinders and handicaps us here on earth. *They (are) before the throne of God, and serve Him day and night within His temple* (Revelation 7:15). And such is the happy prospect of all who have *washed their robes and made them white in the blood of the Lamb* (Revelation 7:14). Until that glorious time though, our petition to God will of necessity be both *Thy kingdom come* and *Thy will be done on earth as it is in heaven.*

Have Thine Own way, Lord
Have Thine Own way
Thou art the Potter
I am the clay
Mould me and make me
After Thy will
While I am waiting
Yielded and still

Have Thine Own way Lord
Have Thine Own way
Hold o'er my being
Absolute sway
Fill with Thy Spirit
Till all shall see
Christ only, always
Living in me.

5

PROVISION
Give us this day our daily bread.

What do we pray for in the fourth petition?

In the fourth petition (which is, GIVE US THIS DAY OUR DAILY BREAD), we pray, that of God's free gift we may receive a competent portion of the good things of this life, and enjoy His blessing with them (Shorter Catechism, Q.108).

The Symmetry of the Six Petitions

There is a beautiful and significant symmetry to the petitions in the 'Lord's Prayer'. The petitions divide exactly. The first three petitions are concerned with God and His glory, and the second three petitions are concerned with ourselves and our needs. Having then prayed for God's honour, kingdom and will, we now petition Him for ourselves, and our need for daily bread, pardon for our sins and deliverance from temptation and evil. From now on, the petitions are concerned with ourselves. We are only human beings, and fallen human beings at that. We cannot get by unless certain of our needs are met.

God in Three Persons, Blessed Trinity

Interestingly, when we pray for ourselves and our needs, using our Saviour's guidelines in the model prayer, we are given a glimpse of the Holy Trinity. The teaching of the Bible is clear. There is only One God, yet there are three Persons in the God-head, the Father, the Son and the Holy Spirit. We are about to pray for provision, pardon and protection. It is God the Father Who provides us with our daily bread. It is by the death of God the Son that our sins are forgiven, and apart from the indwelling ministry of the Holy Spirit, we are powerless against both temptation and the evil one's attacks.

The Fourth Petition

With the acute awareness that God has made us physical, as well as spiritual beings, in this fourth petition, the Lord Jesus encourages us to pray to our Father in heaven: *Give us this day our daily bread.*

This fourth petition reminds us of our total dependence upon God for all things. He is the only truly independent Being that there is. We are totally dependent on Him. He has given us life - our conception was no accident but a divine appointment - and He is the One Who sustains our lives. Looking behind all 'secondary causes', we state that the food we eat which is necessary to sustain our life is inexplicable apart from God's goodness. A farmer may cultivate the soil and sow the seed, but in and of himself he cannot produce the grain which makes our bread. A mother may produce a meal for her family through the careful and skilful manipulation of various ingredients - but she cannot produce these raw ingredients in and of herself. It is God Who is our Maker and Sustainer. We are totally dependent upon Him for the provision of our daily bread:-

Thou dost cause the grass to grow for the cattle, and plants for man to cultivate, that he may bring forth food from the earth, and wine to gladden the heart of man, oil to make his face shine, and bread to strengthen man's heart (Psalm 104:14,15). *The eyes of all look to Thee, and Thou givest them their food in due season. Thou openest Thy hand, Thou satisfiest the desire of every living thing* (Psalm 145:16).

All this being so, it is a good, happy and Biblical practice to 'give thanks' before our meals. This enhances our meal times and acknowledges their ultimate Source. *So, whether you eat or drink, or whatever you do, do all to the glory of God (1 Corinthians 19:31).* A very ancient 'grace' - one which the Lord Jesus would have known - goes 'Blessed art Thou O Lord our God, King of the Universe, Who brings forth bread from the earth.'

One day at a time

Notice that this fourth petition says *Give us <u>this day</u> our <u>daily</u> bread.* The implication here is that we should not look too far ahead, but trust God one day at a time. This ties in with the Lord Jesus's exhortation: *Therefore do not be anxious about tomorrow, for tomorrow will be anxious for itself. Let the day's own trouble be sufficient for the day* (Matthew 6:34). Some of us are very proficient at worrying about what might or might not be in the future! Worrying unduly about tomorrow robs today of its joys. James stated *you do not know about tomorrow* (James 4:14). The Lord does however. Oh to just ask and trust Him for bread for today, and to leave our concerns about tomorrow's bread with Him.

Lessons from the Manna

Valuable lessons on the petition *Give us this day our daily bread* may be gleaned from a consideration of the manna - the bread of heaven which God provided for the people of Israel during their forty years of wandering in the wilderness. *He rained down upon them manna to eat, and gave them the grain of heaven* (Psalm 78:24). This manna was God's gracious provision for His people. The wilderness was a dead and barren place. No food could grow there - but God undertook personally to provide for His people's needs. The Bible records that the manna was:-

i. A divine provision - God provided it.

ii. A daily provision - *Morning by morning they gathered it* (Exodus 16:21). This encouraged the people to trust God for one day at a time -

for *daily bread.* Those who faithlessly hoarded more than one day's supply of manna found *it bred worms and became foul* (Exodus 16:20). Gathering manna was not permitted on the holy Sabbath (seventh) day however, when the people were to be preoccupied with higher, heavenly matters. God's commandments are His enablements, for we read that *On the sixth day they gathered twice as much bread . . . and it did not become foul, and there were no worms in it* (Exodus 16:22,24).

iii. A delightful provision. The daily manna was highly agreeable and suitable to each individual. *He that gathered much had nothing over and he that gathered little had no lack; each gathered according to what he could eat* (Exodus 16:18). This divine and daily provision was certainly delightful to the taste. The Bible tells us that *it was like coriander seed, white, and the taste of it was like wafers made with honey* (Exodus 16:31).

In this way then, God provided sufficient *daily bread* for His people - a provision which they were unable to produce in and of themselves in the harsh, barren wilderness. *They ate the manna, till they came to the border of the land of Canaan* (Exodus 16:35). Joshua 5:12 though states that as soon as the Israelites were out of the wilderness and in the Promised Land, *the manna ceased on the morrow, when they ate of the produce of the land; and the people of Israel had manna no more, but ate of the fruit of the land of Canaan that year.* In the wilderness, God made a miraculous provision. But in Canaan He did not. Why? Because the environment and ecology of Canaan was vastly different from the wilderness. Canaan was *a good and broad land, a land flowing with milk and honey* (Exodus 3:8). Canaan was *a land of wheat and barley, of vines and fig trees and pomegranates, a land of olive trees and honey, a land in which you will eat bread without scarcity* (Deuteronomy 8:8,9). There was no need for a supernatural provision here. If the Israelites worked, and cultivated the land carefully, God saw to it that they would be well provided for, naturally rather than supernaturally. One is as easy as the other to omnipotence.

Daily Bread: Daily Work

There is a principle here. We pray to God for daily bread, for sure. This though is not incompatible with working so that we can provide daily bread for ourselves and our families. Indeed, normally, it is presumptuous not to work and yet still expect God to provide daily bread for us. The Bible stresses the use of 'means' or instruments. For instance, we believe that God saves - but we also believe in the role of human preachers of the Gospel. We pray that God will protect us - but we also lock and bolt our doors at night. We believe that God provides - but we also believe in working for our living in an honest way. *If any one will not work, let him not eat* (2 Thessalonians 3:10). *Let the thief no longer steal, but rather let him labour, doing honest work with his hands, so that he may be able to give to those in need* (Ephesians 4:28).

Need and Greed; Luxury and Poverty; Sufficiency and Contentment

Give us this day our daily bread. Philippians 4:19 assures us *And my God will supply every need of yours according to His riches in glory in Christ Jesus.* Notice though that the verse assures us that God will meet our need and not our greed. Bread comes into the category of need. Bread is in a different category from, for example, fast cars, designer clothes, exotic holidays and restaurant meals. The God Who is infinite in understanding knows our physical and spiritual needs. *Therefore do not be anxious, saying, 'What shall we eat?' or 'What shall we drink?' or 'What shall we wear?' For the Gentiles seek all these things, and your heavenly Father knows that you need them all* (Matthew 6:31,32). Physical luxury has its dangers. It may blind us to the fact that we are more than just physical beings, like animals. *Man shall not live by bread alone, but by every word that proceeds from the mouth of God* (Matthew 4:4). Hardship soon corrects our thinking and drives us back to God. As far as our spiritual life - that is, our walk with God - is concerned, there are dangers to over abundance as much as there is to absolute poverty. Hence the wise petition in Proverbs 30:8,9: *Give me neither poverty nor riches; feed me with the food that is needful for me, lest I be full, and deny Thee, and say, 'Who is the LORD?' or lest I be poor, and steal and profane the name of my God.*

The feverish desire for 'more' is surely one of the engines that drives the world around us. Non conformity to this is a silent but powerful Christian testimony. It reveals by our actions where our hearts and hopes are truly fixed. Inner contentment is possibly one of the neglected Christian virtues today, when Christians perhaps face a greater temptation than ever of jumping on the world's materialistic bandwagon. *There is great gain in godliness with contentment; for we brought nothing into the world, and we cannot take anything out of the world; but if we have food and clothing, with these we shall be content* (1 Timothy 6:6-8).

Give us this day our daily bread. Praying this petition acknowledges our total dependence upon God. *He Himself gives to all men life and breath and everything* (Acts 17:25). The corollary of God's gracious giving is our grateful thanksgiving - acknowledging the gifts and blessing the Giver.

Now thank we all our God
With hearts and hands and voices
Who wondrous things hath done
In Whom this world rejoices
Who from our mother's arms
Hath blessed us on our way
With countless gifts of love
And still is ours today.

6

PARDON

And forgive us our debts, as we also have forgiven our debtors.

What do we pray for in the fifth petition?

In the fifth petition (which is, AND FORGIVE US OUR DEBTS, AS WE FORGIVE OUR DEBTORS), we pray, that God for Christ's sake, would freely pardon all our sins, which we are the rather encouraged to ask, because by His grace we are enabled from the heart to forgive others
(Shorter Catechism, Q. 105).

The Gospel of Forgiveness

The previous petition implies that God is a gracious giver. This petition now implies that God is a merciful forgiver. This is certainly good news. But this good news of divine forgiveness makes no sense at all unless it is considered against the dark background of human sin - a background which makes forgiveness a desperate necessity.

If we break the law of the land, we have to pay a consequent price. Law breaking puts us into the law's debt, and paying the price of this debt could entail a financial fine, community service or even a time in prison.

As God is God, we owe Him total and absolute obedience. When we commit any sin, we break God's Law and so put ourselves in God's debt. There is a penalty to be paid for sin, and it is very high. Unless pardoned, that is, unless our debt of sin can be paid for or written off, we are liable to pay the price for our sins in eternal hell, enduring the wrath of God for all eternity. Sinning against an eternal Being has eternal consequences. *The wages of sin is death* (Romans 6:23).

The Christian Gospel is the glorious news that our sins may be forgiven for Jesus's sake. In Christ, God, in amazing grace and mercy, has cancelled out our sin debt, thus delivering us from suffering its awful, eternal consequences. G.O.S.P.E.L. **G**od's **O**wn **S**on **P**aid **E**very **L**iability. It was on the cross that the sinless Saviour suffered God's punishment for our sins, so that by believing in Him we may go free, and be released from our dreadful debt of sin. The 'Apostle's Creed' has a line which runs: 'I believe in the forgiveness of sins' - and the forgiveness of sins lies at the heart of the Christian Gospel.

To forgive means 'to remit' or 'to refrain from exacting or inflicting a debt or punishment.' If we open the New Testament anywhere, we will find the Good News of forgiveness somewhere:-

Speaking of His impending death on the cross, Jesus explained: *'This is My blood of the new covenant, which is poured out for many for the forgiveness of sins'* (Matthew 26:28).

Writing to the Ephesians, Paul rejoiced: *In Him we have redemption through His blood, the forgiveness of our trespasses, according to the riches of His grace* (Ephesians 1:7).

Writing to the Colossians, Paul explained and exclaimed that God in Christ on the cross has *forgiven us all our trespasses, having cancelled the bond (IOU) which stood against us with its legal demands; this He set aside, nailing it to the cross* (Colossians 2:13,14).

1 John contains the mature reflections of the Apostle John - perhaps one of the closest human beings to Jesus ever. Yet in this letter, John adamantly reminds us of the Christian basics: *I am writing to you, little children, because your sins are forgiven for His sake* (1 John 2:12).

I will sing of my Redeemer
And His wondrous love to me
On the cruel cross He suffered
From the curse to set me free

Sing, O sing, of my Redeemer!
With His blood He purchased me
On the cross He sealed my pardon
Paid the debt and made me free.

Why do we pray for forgiveness?

The question is, if our sins have been forever forgiven, because of the finished Work of Christ at Calvary, why do Christians still need to pray for forgiveness? The prayer which we are considering is a distinctively Christian prayer. Praying it is the prerogative of Christians alone. Yet Christians - a forgiven people - are, paradoxically, encouraged to pray *Forgive us our debts. . .*

The answer is a simple one. It is because we are still prone to sin, and will be until we are glorified. Hence we need to confess our sins daily, and seek God's continued pardon. Writing to Christians, John says *If we say we have no sin we deceive ourselves and the truth is not in us. If we confess our sins He is faithful and just, and will forgive our sins and cleanse us from all unrighteousness* (1 John 1:8,9).

Standing and state

A way of understanding this, is by comparing a Christian's standing and state. Think of a child in a family. His status as a child is secure and assured. Sometimes though he misbehaves. His misbehaviour puts a cloud between him and his parents until he apologises for what he has done. It is similar in the Christian life. In amazing grace God has adopted us into His family for ever. Nothing can change this high status. Once born again we cannot be unborn. Yet, when we sin, we mar our enjoyment of our fellowship with God which is our new birthright. Hence, we need to humbly confess our sins to God. *Forgive us our debts* and our fellowship with God is restored.

An illustration from the Gospels of having been forgiven and yet, paradoxically, still needing forgiveness, may be gleaned from John 13. In John 13 we read about an incident of infinite condescension, for in this chapter we see the Lord Jesus taking upon Himself the role of the lowest slave, and stooping down to wash His disciples' feet. In John 13:10 Jesus says to Peter: *'He who has bathed does not need to wash, except for his feet, but he is clean all over.'*

Consider going out for the evening in the Israel of the first century. You would wash and change, and then walk to your location. In walking though, you would soil your feet. Open toed sandals were the norm then, and the roads were dusty. Hence a slave would obligingly wash your feet on arrival at your location. An overall wash was not necessary - but a foot wash was.

Apply this to our walk to heaven. We have been made ready for this glorious location by *the washing of regeneration and renewal in the Holy Spirit* (Titus 3:5). Hence, we are *clean all over.* Yet, in walking through this world, we 'soil our feet.' The sin without and the sin within spoil our fellowship with God which is our highest joy. And so we pray: *And forgive us our trespasses . . .*

Forgiven and Forgiving

The complete line of the fourth petition reads *And forgive us our debts, as we also have forgiven our debtors.* Similarly, just after the Lord Jesus had given this matchless prayer, He stated *For if you forgive men their trespasses, your heavenly Father also will forgive you; but if you do not forgive men their trespasses, neither will your Father forgive your trespasses* (Matthew 6:14,15). These verses have all been open to much misinterpretation. Some have considered that our eternal spiritual well being - God's forgiveness of us - is conditional upon our forgiveness of others. If this were indeed so - which it isn't - then salvation would be based on human works and not divine grace. And if this were so - which it isn't - there would be no Gospel at all.

We know from the Bible though, that the forgiveness of our sins rests, not on our attitude to others, but on the redeeming cross-work of the Lord Jesus Christ. Hence, we forgive others because God has forgiven us. We do not forgive others to earn God's favour, for salvation is solely by God's grace. We forgive because we have already received God's favour and forgiveness. Our forgiving attitude is then a fruit of salvation, not a root of our salvation. Paul brings all this out in the following verses, where he exhorts believers to act on and work out their Christian salvation:-

Be kind to one another, tender-hearted, forgiving one another, as God in Christ forgave you (Ephesians 4:32).

. . . forbearing one another and, if one has a complaint against another, forgiving each other; as the Lord has forgiven you, so you also must forgive (Colossians 3:13).

The problem of bitterness and resentment

Personal bitterness is one of the most destructive forces in the world. Some of us still carry severe hurts and psychological scars from the treatment we received from others in the past. How do we deal with these? How do we avoid being 'eaten up' by resentment? The antidote is surely to consider God's amazing grace to us in Christ. Our sin offended Him, and sinning against Almighty God Himself could not be more serious. Yet God in Christ has freely pardoned all our sins. When we consider and rejoice in God's free forgiveness of us, it is highly inconsistent, even hypocritical, for us to then go and hold grudges against others. As we have been forgiven, so we must now forgive. He has cancelled our huge debt, so how then can we not write off the lesser debts we feel that others owe to us?

To illustrate the matter of being forgiven and then forgiving others as a consequence, the Lord Jesus once told a graphic, 'human interest' parable. It is found in Matthew 18:23 ff., and quoted now in full:-

'Therefore the kingdom of heaven may be compared to a king who wanted to settle accounts with his servants. When he began the reckoning, one was brought to him who owed him ten thousand talents; and as he could not pay, his lord ordered him to be sold, with his wife and children and all that he had, and payment to be made. So the servant fell on his knees, imploring him, 'Lord, have patience with me, and I will pay you everything.' And out of pity for him the lord of that servant released him and forgave him the debt. But that same servant, as he went out, came upon one of his fellow servants who owed him a hundred denarii; and seizing him by the throat he said, 'Pay what you owe.' So his fellow servant fell down and besought him, 'Have patience with me,

and I will pay you.' He refused and went and put him in prison till he should pay the debt. When his fellow servants saw what had taken place, they were greatly distressed, and they went and reported to their lord all that had taken place. Then his lord summoned him and said to him, 'You wicked servant! I forgave you all that debt because you besought me; and should not you have had mercy on your fellow servant, as I had mercy on you?' And in anger his lord delivered him to the jailers, till he should pay all his debt. So also my heavenly Father will do to every one of you, if you do not forgive your brother from the heart.'

And forgive us our debts, as we also forgive our debtors. In this line more than any, we see why the title 'The Lord's Prayer' is a misnomer. The sinless Son of God certainly had no need to pray this petition. He *knew no sin* (2 Corinthians 5:21). *He committed no sin* (1 Peter 2:22). *In Him there is no sin* (1 John 3:5). We though, as His disciples, will need to pray it daily, this side of eternity. Let us then rejoice in God's forgiveness - *the blood of Jesus His Son cleanses us from all sin* (1 John 1:7). God has been merciful to us and blessed us. Let us also seek His grace to show mercy to others. As He has forgiven us, let us seek His grace that we will not nurse grudges against those who have offended us. God's blessings bring responsibilities as well. If we are truly rejoicing in the forgiveness of our sins through the death of Christ, the onus is now on us to forgive.

7

PROTECTION

And lead us not into temptation, but deliver us from evil.

What do we pray for in the sixth petition?

In the sixth petition (which is, AND LEAD US NOT INTO TEMPTATION, BUT DELIVER US FROM EVIL) we pray that God would either keep us from being tempted to sin, or support and deliver us when we are tempted (*Shorter Catechism*, Q.106).

Introduction

When we pray for our daily bread, we acknowledge our need and total dependence on God for all things. Likewise, when we pray that God will forgive us our trespasses, we acknowledge that we are sinners by nature and practice, and our earthly and eternal well-being totally depends upon His forgiveness. Here now though, in this sixth petition, by praying for deliverance from temptation and evil, we acknowledge our spiritual weakness, vulnerability and our proneness to fall, and our desperate need for divine protection. With His intimate knowledge of our human frame, the Lord Jesus exhorts and encourages us to pray: *And lead us not into temptation, but deliver us from evil.*

Whilst ever we are in this world, we will need the help of God if we are to please God. Whilst ever we are in this world, we will also need the help of God if we are not to displease God. All Christians are the same here. The most recent convert and the maturest saint and all in-between share an equal need of God's indwelling Holy Spirit, if they are not to succumb to doing that which displeases the Lord. Having just prayed for the forgiveness of our sins, we now pray that the Lord would deliver us from falling into sin in the future.

Hard Testing

This petition *And lead us not into temptation* can be interpreted in more than one way. The Greek word 'peirasmos', meaning 'temptation', can also be translated as 'hard testing.' Think of an athlete - say a middle distance runner - under the guidance of an expert coach. The coach knows all about training, and has to give an appropriate schedule to the athlete under his charge. The schedule is personally designed so that it provides just enough effort, resistance and difficulty for the runner to improve, that is, to strengthen the necessary muscles and increase the heart and lung capacity needed for getting swiftly around the track. If the training is not hard enough, the athlete regresses in form. Conversely, over training leads to the athlete getting injured.

In praying *And lead us not into hard testing* therefore, we are praying to our Father 'Go easy on me.' 'Please provide only those trials which You know are necessary for my spiritual improvement - those difficulties which deepen my faith in You, and enable me to learn those needed lessons in human sympathy.'

If only we could see all of our trials, difficulties and hardships as coming from the hand of our loving Father in heaven. He is training us for excellence! Knowing Him means that nothing haphazard enters our lives. *From Him and through Him and to Him are all things* (Romans 11:36). *We know that in everything God works for good with those who love Him, who are called according to His purpose* (Romans 8:28).

On the authority of the Bible, we may state that our Father in heaven will never test and try us beyond our personal capacity. He controls the heat, for sure, but He also controls the thermostat! *For He knows our frame; He remembers that we are dust* (Psalm 103:14).

All sufficient grace

1 Corinthians 10:13 contains an all embracing promise that the Lord God will give us the strength to cope with whatever He sends our way. If He does not lighten our load, He will certainly give us a stronger back! *No temptation (hard testing) has overtaken you that is not common to man. God is faithful, and He will not let you be tempted* (tested) *beyond your strength, but with the temptation will also provide the way of escape, that you may be able to endure it.*

2 Corinthians 12:7 ff. describes a severe trial faced by the Apostle Paul. Finding himself in excruciating pain, Paul naturally prayed for God's deliverance. The Lord answered his prayer. He answered it though, not by removing the trial, but by giving Paul greater coping strength. God's promise to Paul, and to you and me in our trials and tribulations is the same: *My grace is sufficient for you* (2 Corinthians 12:9).

> He giveth more grace when the burdens grow greater
> He sendeth more strength when the labours increase
> To added affliction He addeth His mercy
> To multiplied trials His multiplied peace
>
> His love has no limit
> His grace has no measure
> His power has no boundary known unto men
> For out of His infinite riches in Jesus
> He giveth, and giveth and giveth again.

Temptation to Sin

The usual way of understanding the petition *And lead us not into temptation* concerns that of being tempted to sin. It is a serious matter, for *each person is tempted when he is lured and enticed by his own desire. Then desire when it has conceived gives birth to sin; and sin when it is full-grown brings forth death* (James 1:14,15).

The petition therefore has an underlying concern that we shun anything and everything which would spoil our fellowship with God, dishonour His Name and bring the cause of Christ into disrepute. Church history is littered with those who brought disgrace on themselves and reproach on the name of Christ. The petition is a sincere prayer that we may not be numbered among this roll of dishonour. We are all made of the same flesh and blood, and we all share the same fallen human nature which is capable of the most heinous sins. *Look to yourself, lest you too be tempted* (Galatians 6:1). Surely, no Christian has ever set out to deliberately blot his copy book. *Therefore let any one who thinks that he stands take heed lest he fall* (1 Corinthians 10:12).

The petition *And lead us not into temptation* needs careful, and Scriptural interpretation. Perish the thought that a thrice holy God could ever tempt us to sin against Him! James 1:13,14 reads: *Let no one say when he is tempted, 'I am tempted by God', for God cannot be tempted with evil and He Himself tempts no one; but each person is tempted when he is lured and enticed by his own desire.*

Sadly, we have to take full responsibility for our sinful actions. Those who blame the devil, their genes, their environment or even their hormones, in truth, cannot fool their own guilty conscience. Acknowledging God's sovereign Lordship over the circumstances of our lives though - as well as our proneness to sin - we pray *Lead us not into temptation.* Here we are praying that God will prevent us from being brought into those situations and circumstances outside of us which are such that the temptation to do something which God forbids is greater than our power to resist. We are praying that we will not make shipwreck of our Faith. Imagine the horror if our fallen nature and baser desires went unchecked and we were given a circumstance in which they could have unrestricted reign . . . *Lead us not into temptation.* Perhaps eternity alone will reveal the number of times when could God could have said to us *It was I who kept you from sinning against Me* (Genesis 20:6).

As we have an internal enemy, which seeks to spoil our fellowship with God, we are impelled to pray *lead us not into temptation.* Biblical realism though also acknowledges that we have an infernal enemy as well as an internal one. As well as having to do battle with our fallen inner nature, we also have to do battle with one who smarts that we are now no longer under his sway. There is a Devil. We cannot claim to be Bible-believing Christians if we deny the existence of a personal Devil - referred to variously as the Devil, Satan, our Adversary and the Evil One. The Evil One would like to do all that is in his mighty, but limited power and cunning to wreck our spiritual lives. This being so, the Lord Jesus taught that our prayers should include this petition for divine protection: *Deliver us from the Evil One.*

Our Adversary the Devil

It is immaterial whether we translate the second half of the sixth petition *deliver us from evil* or *deliver us from the Evil One.* Scripture is clear. Whether we like it or not, there is a personal Devil - *the* Evil One - a sinister being who has nothing but evil designs on our souls. Hence Peter warned: *Be sober, be watchful. Your adversary the devil prowls around like a roaring lion, seeking some one to devour* (1 Peter 5:8). The Devil is mighty - far mightier than us - but he is not all mighty. Hence it is to the Almighty that we pray *deliver us from the evil one.* Paul warned against *the wiles of the devil* (Ephesians 6:11). He certainly is wily, and knows our weak points and how to play on them. Yet he is no match for the One to Whom we pray for help and deliverance. Our God is One *abundant in power Whose understanding is beyond measure* (Psalm 147:5).

Christians then should be aware and beware of the Evil One. We should neither over nor under estimate his power and guile. In the ministry of the Lord Jesus, Satan received a severe blow, disabling his power. *The reason the Son of God appeared was to destroy the works of the devil* (1 John 3:8). *He disarmed the principalities and powers and made a public example of them, triumphing over them in Him* (Colossians 2:15).

And lead us not into temptation, but deliver us from evil. This sixth petition acknowledges our weakness and proneness to fall into temptation, as it also acknowledges that there is an enemy of our souls, who is greater than we are, left to our own devices. How we need to pray this petition. How we are in need of the help of both the Word of God and the Spirit of God. *I have laid up Thy Word in my heart, that I might not sin against Thee* (Psalm 119:11). *He Who is in you is greater than he who is in the world* (1 John 4:4).

The coming answer to our prayers

Temptation and the Devil are our worst enemies, as they both seek to rob us of the greatest blessing of all. They both seek to spoil the fellowship with God which is our chief end. It is vital therefore to pray for deliverance from them both. The good news is that one day our prayers will be fully answered. *The Lord will rescue me from every evil and save me for His heavenly kingdom. To Him be the glory for ever and ever. Amen.* (2 Timothy 4:18).

Our present struggles are not for ever. One day, we will be immune from temptation, and out of the devil's reach, and able to enjoy unblemished fellowship with God for all eternity. Scripture holds out this certain prospect for all who belong to Jesus. It is a hope to encourage us to 'keep on keeping on' - keeping on praying, and keeping on battling against the evil within and without. Heaven contains *the spirits of just men made perfect* (Hebrews 12:23). John assures us that one day *we shall be like Him* (1 John 3:2). Paul assures us that *The God of peace will soon crush Satan under your feet* (Romans 16:20).

Battling against sin and Satan is a struggle from which no Christian is exempt. But *the sufferings of this present time are not worth comparing with the glory that is to be revealed to us* (Romans 8:18). Our confidence is in the God to Whom we pray *And lead us not into temptation, but deliver us from evil.* For *the Lord is faithful; He will strengthen you and guard you from evil* (2 Thessalonians 3:3).

8

PRAISE

*For Thine is the kingdom and the power and the glory,
for ever. Amen*

What doth the conclusion of the Lord's Prayer teach us?

*The conclusion of the Lord's Prayer (which is, FOR THINE IS
THE KINGDOM, AND THE POWER, AND THE GLORY,
FOR EVER, AMEN) teacheth us to take our encouragement in
prayer from God only, and in our prayers to praise Him, ascribing
kingdom, power, and glory to Him. And in testimony of our
desire, and assurance to be heard, we say, Amen*
(*Shorter Catechism*, Q. 107).

And Finally

We come now, finally, to consider the ending to the 'Lord's Prayer.' The
perfect prayer concludes with this magnificent ascription of praise to

the One Who alone is worth of such praise, and that for ever. In this praise our prayer is brought to a fitting conclusion and climax.

> Give to our God immortal praise
> Mercy and truth are all His ways
> Wonders of grace to God belong
> Repeat His mercies in your song

> Give to the Lord of lords renown
> The King of kings with glory crown
> His mercies ever shall endure
> When lords and kings are known no more.

Whether these words *For Thine is the kingdom and the power and the glory, for ever. Amen* were actually part of the Lord's original teaching on prayer is debated. But what cannot be denied is just how in-tune and in-line with the whole Bible is the worship here offered. If we know our Bibles, we can hear distinct echoes of the praise offered once by king David here, at the time he made preparations for the building of the Temple - a building which Solomon his son would eventually see built. In 1 Chronicles 29:10 ff. David exclaimed:-

Blessed art Thou, O LORD, the God of Israel our father, for ever and ever. Thine, O LORD, is the greatness, and the power, and the glory, and the victory, and the majesty; for all that is in the heavens and in the earth is Thine; Thine is the kingdom, O LORD, and Thou art exalted as head above all . . . And now we thank Thee, our God, and praise Thy glorious name.

What are we in relation to such matchless, unchallengeable kingship, limitless in power and incomparable in glory? Before God, our true place is in the dust. Yet what great encouragement this awareness of God's 'God-ness' gives us. Our prayers may be weak and imperfect for sure - but we pray to One Who is perfect! Our God is perfect, and absolute in sovereign power. Nothing can hinder Him from answering our prayers when they are made with a mind for our true well being and His eternal glory. Examining this concluding praise a little more closely, we see:-

1. The Kingdom is God's

Thine is the kingdom. . . . The total and absolute sovereignty of God is a theme which runs throughout the Bible. *The LORD reigns; He is robed in majesty; the LORD is robed, He is girded with strength* (Psalm 93:1). In dealing with God we are dealing with the Royal Power. *For the LORD, the Most High is terrible, a great king over all the earth* (Psalm 47:2). *Hallelujah! For the Lord our God the Almighty reigns* (Revelation 19:6).

Imagine a school boy for a moment. Poor fellow, he is having difficulty with his homework. He needs help. He seeks it, but in a somewhat audacious way. He bypasses his parents, his subject teacher, his form teacher and his head master, and writes a letter explaining his problem directly to the Secretary of State for Education! In praying to God, we are taking our difficulties and needs right 'to the top'. There is no higher authority than the King of kings and Lord of lords. *Your God reigns* (Isaiah 52:7). There is none greater than God. He is *the Most High* (Psalm 91:1).

O worship the King, all glorious above
O gratefully sing His power and His love
Our shield and defender, the ancient of days
Pavilioned in splendour, and girded with praise.

2. The Power is God's

Thine is the . . . power . . . The God and Father of our Lord Jesus Christ is as infinite in power as He is in love.

How good is the God we adore
Our faithful unchangeable Friend!
His love is as great as His power
And knows neither measure nor end.

Thine is the . . . power . . . Love without power would be a love that is well meaning but ineffectual. Power without love would be a fearsome brutality. But as regards our Father in heaven, 'His love is as great as His power.' *Thine is . . . the power.*

A meditation on and an awareness of God's power will increase our incentive to pray. It is sometimes said that 'prayer changes things.' This is only so because God is able to change things. He is able to change things because He is infinite in power. To think that He condescends to put His infinite power at our disposal staggers belief, but the testimony of Scripture tells us that this is so. Note the references to both God's tenderness and power - or even 'tender power' - all within a few lines of the following Psalms:-

He heals the brokenhearted, and binds up their wounds. He determines the number of the stars, He gives to all of them their names. Great is our LORD, and abundant in power; His understanding is beyond measure. The LORD lifts up the downtrodden . . . (Psalm 147:3 ff.).

To Him Who by understanding made the heavens . . .Who spread out the earth upon the waters . . . Who made the great lights . . . the sun to rule over the day . . . the moon and stars to rule over the night . . . It is He who remembered us in our low estate, for His steadfast love endures for ever (Psalm 136:5, 6, 7, 8, 23).

Recalling God's power then reminds us that no need or difficulty or seeming impossibility of ours is too great Him. We need never despair. Our seemingly insoluable problems can be easily solved by God. His is the power. We may be weak, but our Father is Almighty. *Ah Lord God! It is Thou who hast made the heavens and the earth by Thy great power and by Thy outstretched arm! Nothing is too hard for Thee* (Jeremiah 32:17). *For with God nothing will be impossible* (Luke 1:37).

In praying to God, we are praying to the ultimate power. Prayer is a tapping into God's power and a laying hold of God's willingness. Appearances deceive. The most powerful force on earth is at work when . . . one of God's children kneels down to pray. When we pray in the will of God, no natural or supernatural force can hinder omnipotence from answering our prayer. *I know that Thou canst do all things, and that no purpose of Thine can be thwarted* (Job 42:2).

Finally, the perfect prayer also reminds us that:-

3. The Glory is God's

Thine is . . . the glory, for ever and ever. Amen. We tend to think of salvation in terms of the great personal blessings that it brings to the human soul. And it certainly does! Even the blessings of personal salvation however are secondary in relation to the glory of God. *We who have first hoped in Christ have been destined and appointed to live for the praise of His glory* (Ephesians 1:12). The glory of God and the God of glory could not be more all-embracing. Truth be told, the true and ultimate goal of absolutely everything is the unsurpassed and unsurpassable, total, absolute and indescribable glory of the all glorious God. *Not to us, O LORD, not to us, but to Thy name give glory* (Psalm 115:1).

Mere words fail us when we consider the glory of God. The dictionary defines 'glory' using words such as 'exalted renown, fame, resplendent majesty, radiance, beauty.' Such words are useful in their sphere, but we cannot begin to define or encapsulate the surpassing glory of the one true God. He is altogether different, unique and in a category of His Own. He once said of Himself: *I am the LORD, that is My name; my glory I give to no other* (Isaiah 42:8). Men may have their little moments of relative glory - perhaps it in the sporting, artistic, commercial or political fields. But such 'glory' is very transient. It soon passes. The song of Scripture though is *Glory to God in the highest* (Luke 2:14). *To Him be glory for ever. Amen* (Romans 11:36). God's is the eternal, untarnished, undiminished glory of *the blessed and only Sovereign, the King of kings and Lord of lords, Who alone has immortality and dwells in unapproachable light, Whom no man has ever seen or can see. To Him be honour and eternal dominion. Amen* (1 Timothy 6:15,16).

Glory to God! And may our prayers in general, and our praying of this special 'Lord's Prayer' in particular hasten that coming glorious day when God's purposes of grace and glory will be complete, and *the earth will be filled with the knowledge of the glory of the LORD, as the waters cover the sea* (Habakkuk 2:14). As evidence of our sincerity we thus say 'Amen' - 'It is so', 'May it be so', 'Let it be so.'

Amen! May it be so in due course, in the all-wise plan and time-scale of the God *Who hearest prayer* (Psalm 65:2). To *the only wise God be glory for ever more through Jesus Christ! Amen* (Romans 16:27).

SOLI DEO GLORIA

EPILOGUE

Lord, teach us to pray (Luke 11:1)

Lord, teach us how to pray aright
With reverence and with fear
Though dust and ashes in Thy sight
We may, we must draw near

We perish if we cease from prayer
O grant us power to pray
And when to meet Thee we prepare
Lord, meet us by the way

Give deep humility, the sense
Of godly sorrow give
A strong desiring confidence
To hear Thy voice and live

Faith in the only sacrifice
That can for sin atone
To build our hopes, to fix our eyes
On Christ, on Christ alone

Patience to watch and wait and weep
Though mercy long delay
Courage, our fainting souls to keep
And trust Thee, though Thou slay

Give these and then Thy will be done
Thus strengthened with all might
We through Thy Spirit and Thy Son
Shall pray, and pray aright.

(James Montgomery 1771-1854)